FOR ORGANS, PIANOS & ELECTRONIC KEYBOARDS

E-Z PLAY TODAY 108

CLASSIC THEMES
Edición Inglesa/Española

T0045108

E-Z Play TODAY is designed for you!

- All songs are arranged for use with all major brand organs.
- Special chord notation for SINGLE KEY CHORDS... TRIAD CHORDS... and STANDARD CHORD POSITIONS.
- MUSIC BASICS on page 46 — a quick review of the E-Z Play TODAY music notation.
- The result... INSTANT PLAYING ENJOYMENT!

E-Z Play TODAY, ha sido especialmente diseñado para usted!

- Todas las canciones han sido arregladas para ser interpretadas en cualquier órgano de marca conocida.
- Notaciones especiales para ACORDES DE UNA TECLA... ACORDE DE TRES NOTAS... y POSICIONES STANDARD DE ACORDE.
- FUNDAMENTALES DE MUSICA en la pagina 46 ofrece una revisión rápida de la notación de música Método simple de Tocar.
- El resultado... DISFRUTE TOCANDO INSTANTANEAMENTE.

Contents

2 Ave Maria
5 Barcarolle
8 Etude, Opus 10 #3
10 Für Elise
12 Hallelujah Chorus
14 Jesu, Joy Of Man's Desiring
16 Largo (From New World Symphony)
19 Liebestraum
24 Minuet in G
25 Moonlight Sonata
28 Polonaise, Opus 53
30 Sonata No. 8 in C Minor
32 Sonata Pastoral
34 Theme From Swan Lake
36 Theme From The Four Seasons
39 Unfinished Symphony
40 Waltz Of The Flowers
45 Wedding March

46 Music Basics
48 Chord Speller

Indice

12 ¡Aleluya! De "El Mesías"
32 Andante De La Sonata Pastoral
2 Ave Maria
5 Barcarola
40 Cascanueces
25 Claro De Luna
34 El Lago De Los Cisnes
8 Etude, Opus 10 #3
14 Jesus, Alegria De Los Hombres
30 La Bella Durmiente
16 Largo—De La Sinfonia Del Nuevo Mundo
36 Las Cuatro Estaciones
45 Marcha Nupcial
39 Melodia Inacabada
24 Minueto
10 Para Elisa
28 Polenesa
30 Sonata Patética
19 Sueno De Amor

46 Fundamentales de Musica
48 Cuadro Descriptivo de Acordes

HAL•LEONARD CORPORATION
7777 W. BLUEMOUND RD. P.O. BOX 13819 MILWAUKEE, WI 53213

Ave Maria

Registration 4

Bach/Gounod

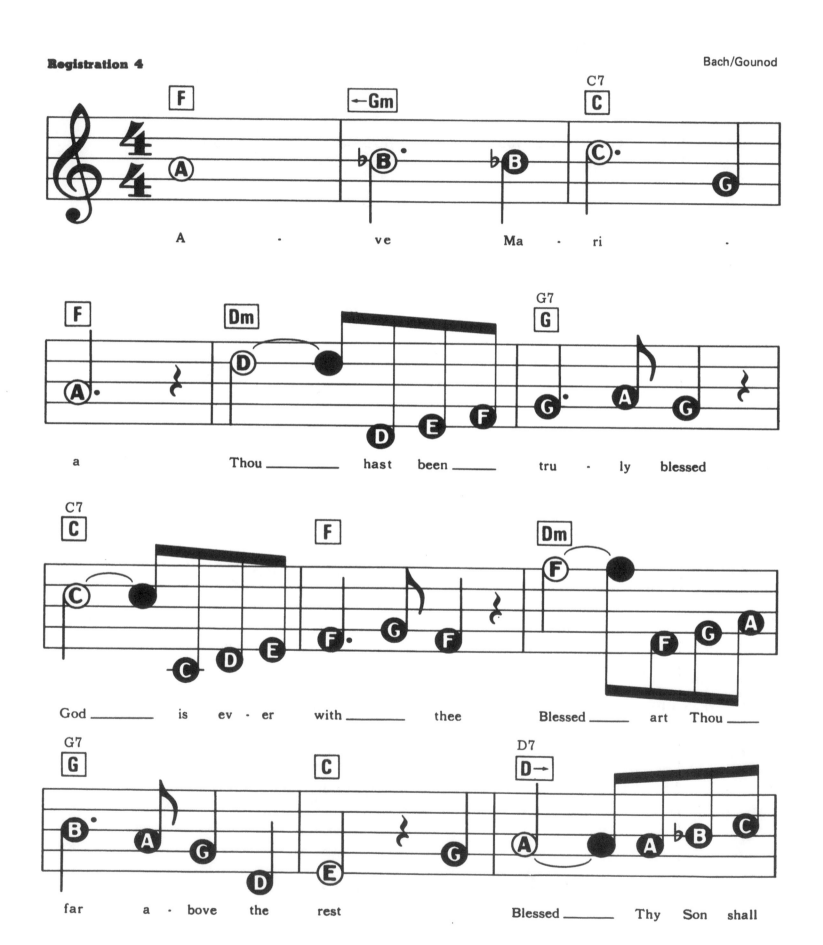

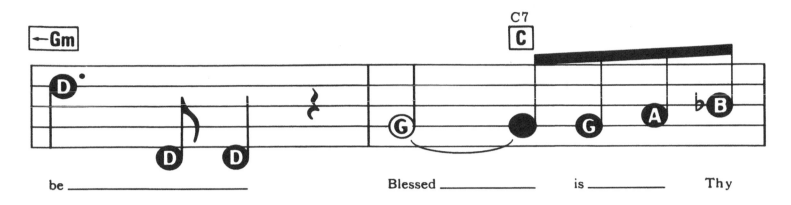

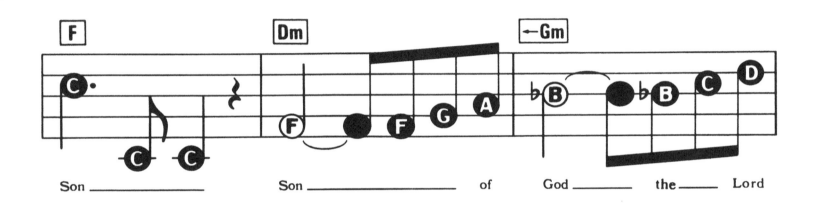

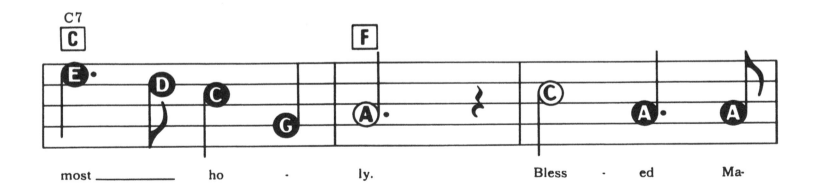

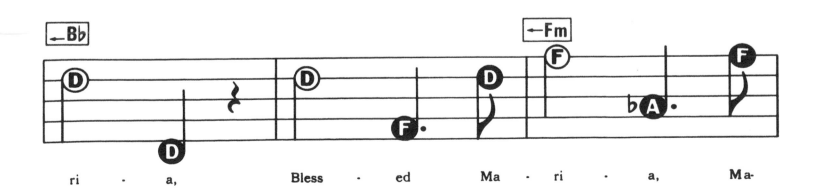

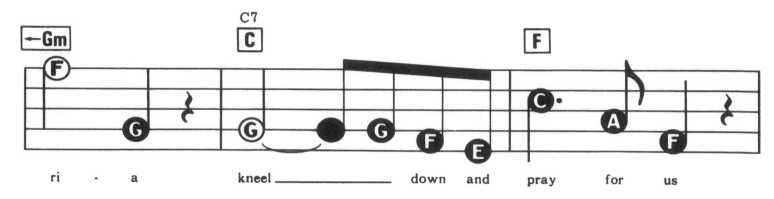

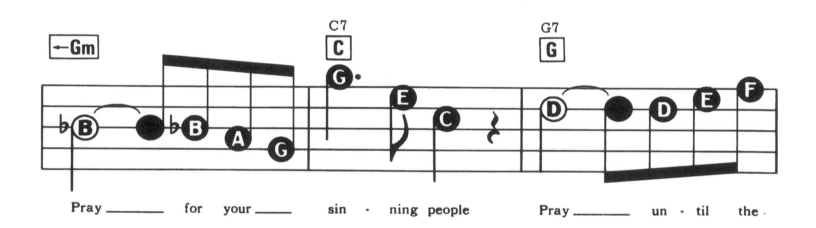

ri - a   kneel _____ down and   pray   for   us

Pray _____ for your _____ sin · ning people   Pray _____ un · til   the ·

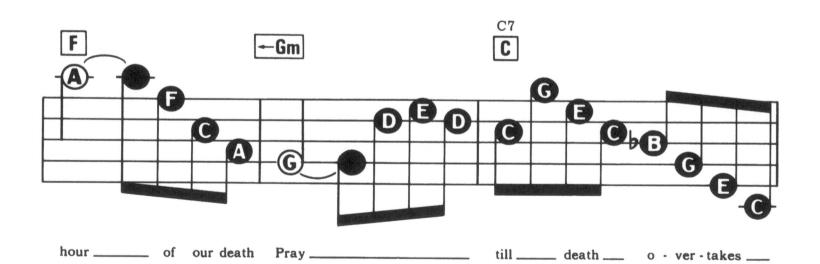

hour _____ of our death Pray _____ till _____ death ____ o · ver · takes _____

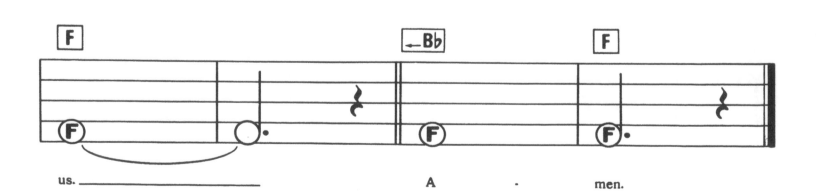

us. _____   A · men.

Barcarolle
(Barcarola)

Registration 4

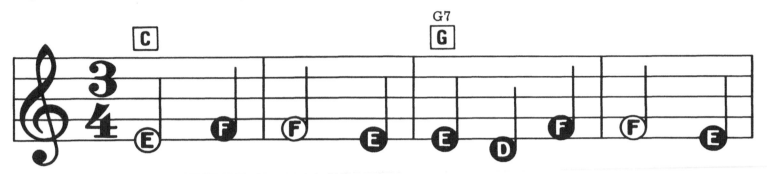

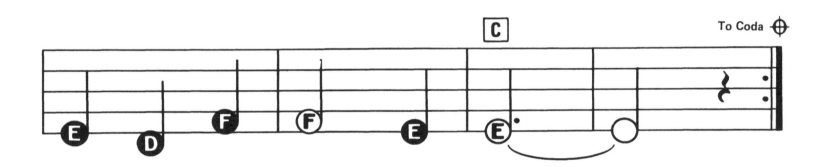

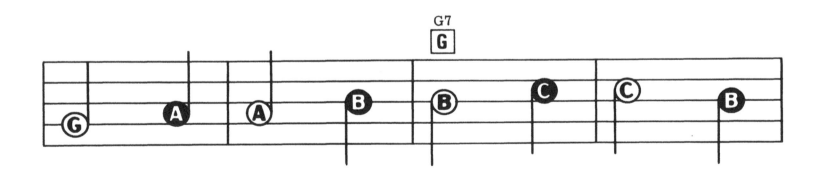

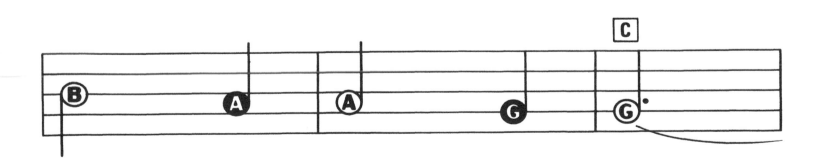

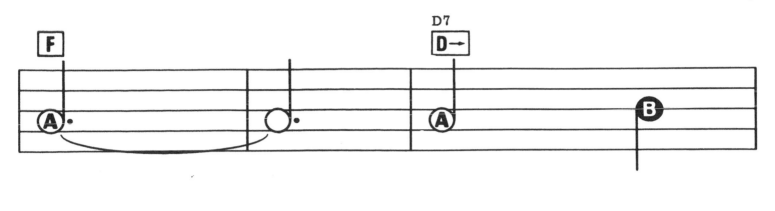

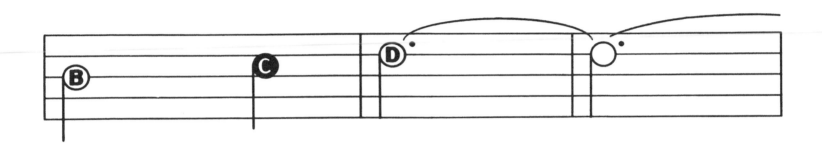

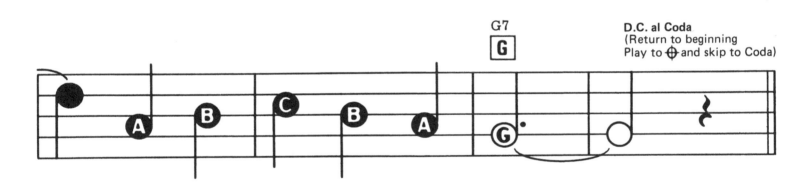

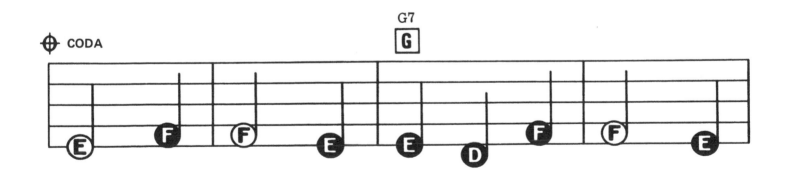

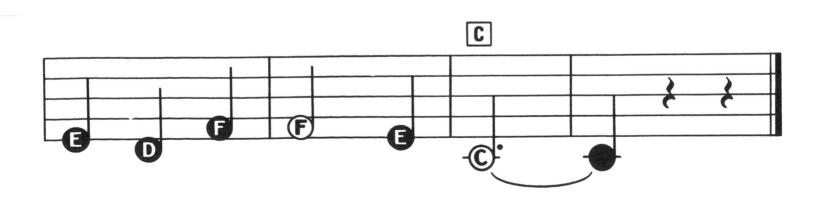

Etude, Opus 10#3

F. Chopin

Registration 8

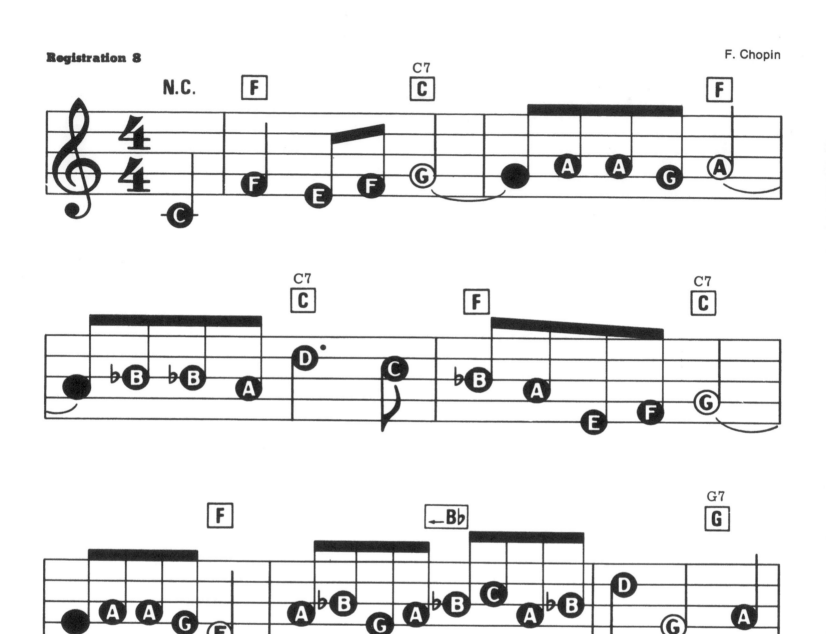

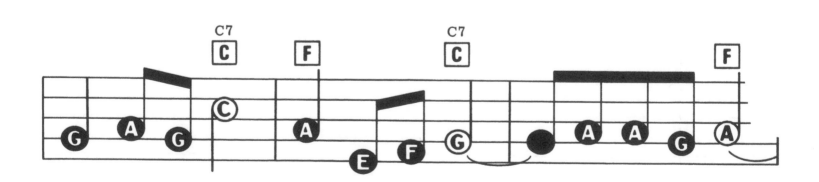

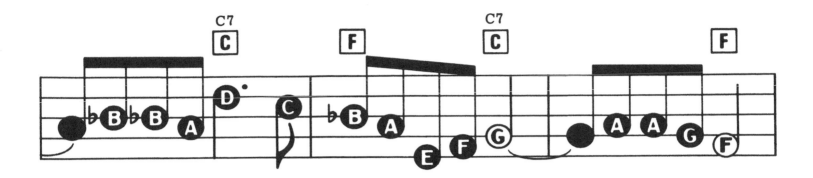

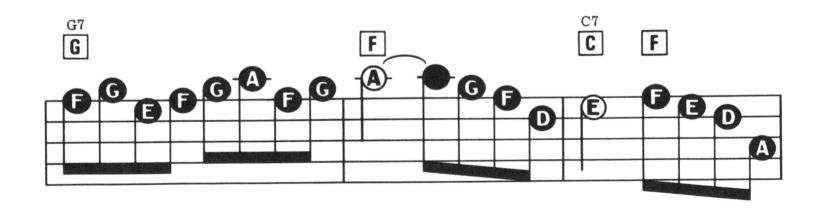

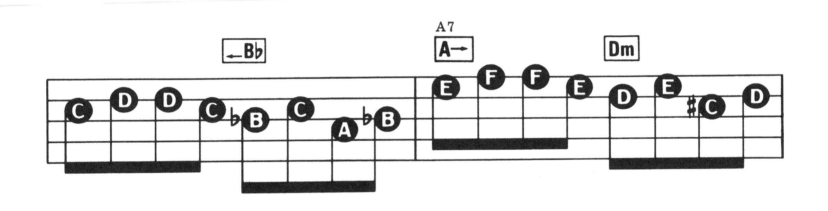

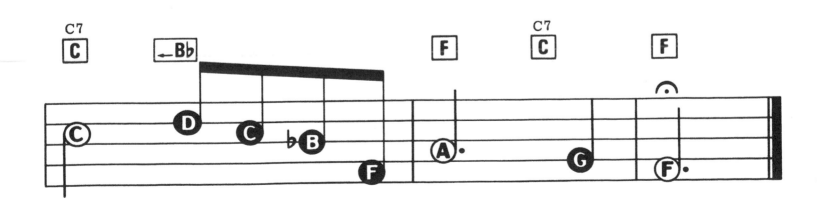

9

Für Elise
(Para Elisa)

Registration 6

Ludwig von Beethoven

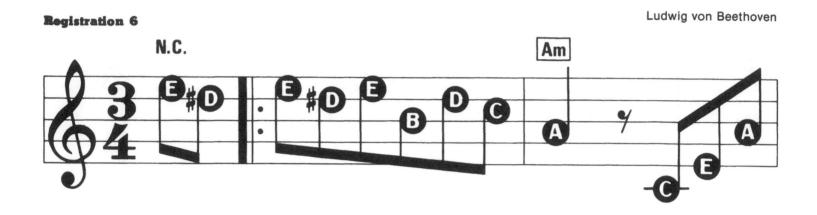

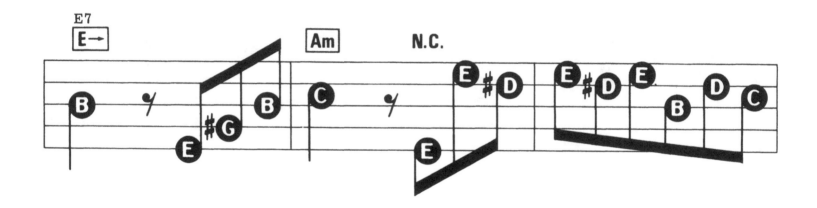

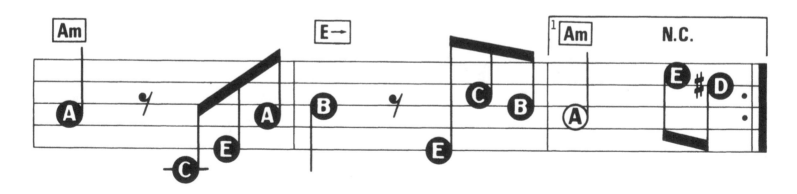

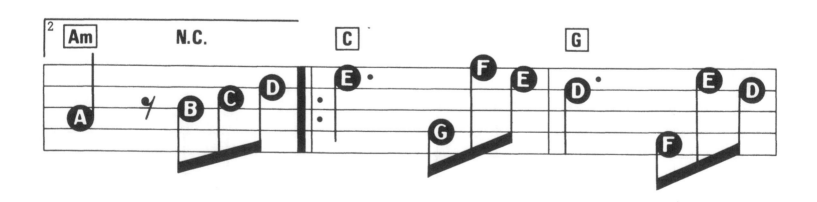

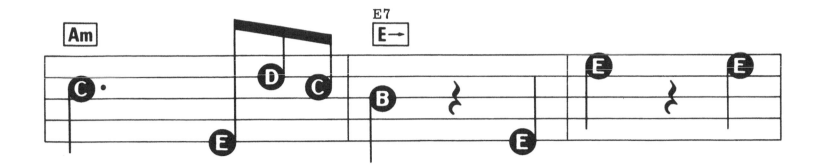

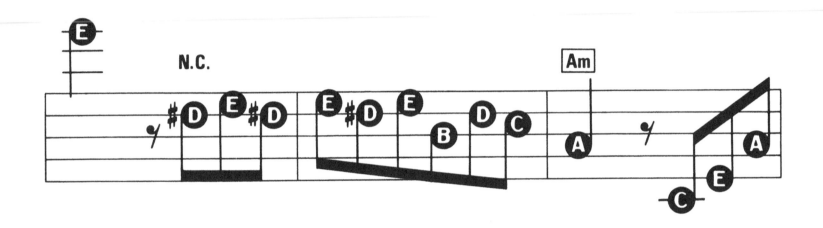

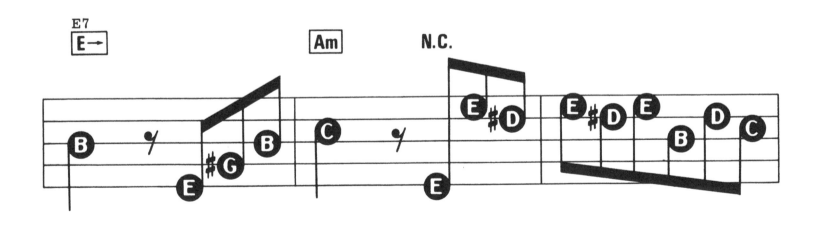

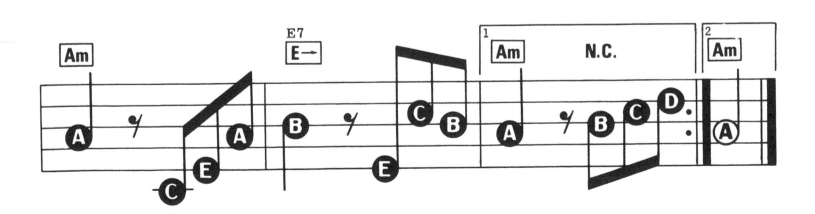

Hallelujah Chorus
(¡Aleluya! de "El Mesías")

Registration 4

G.F. Handel

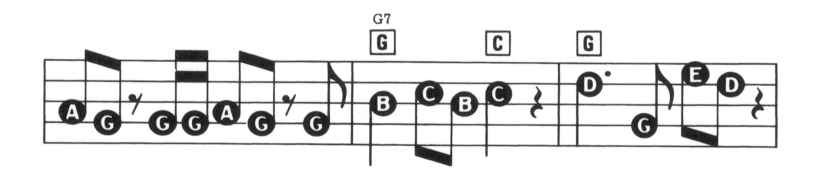

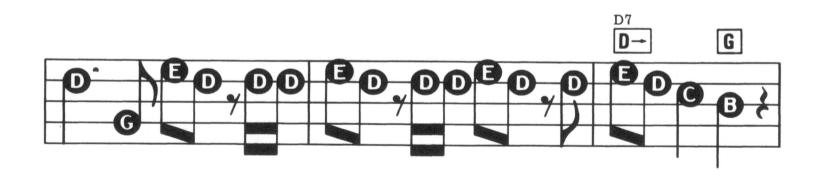

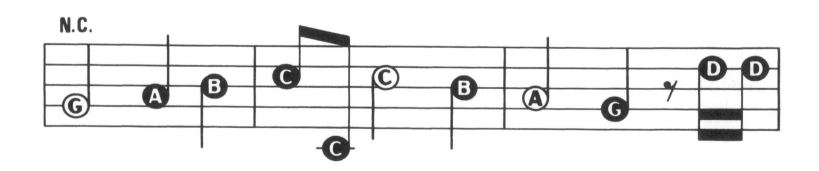

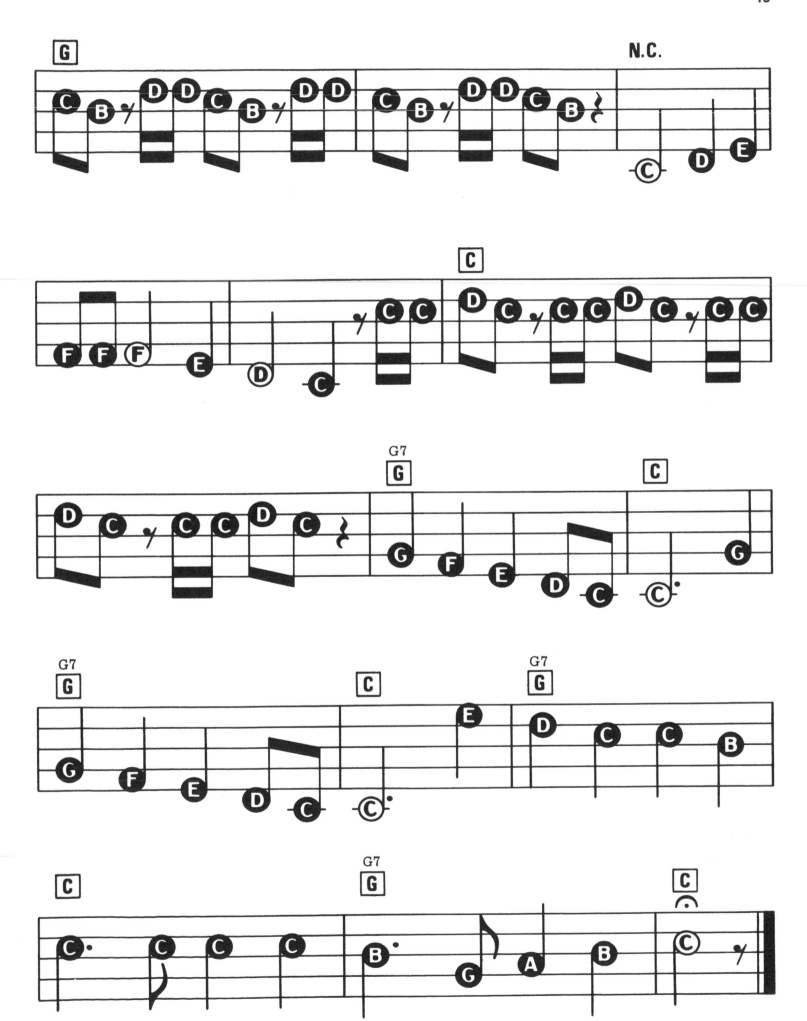

Jesu, Joy Of Man's Desiring
(Jesús, Alegria de los Hombres)

J.S. Bach

Registration 2

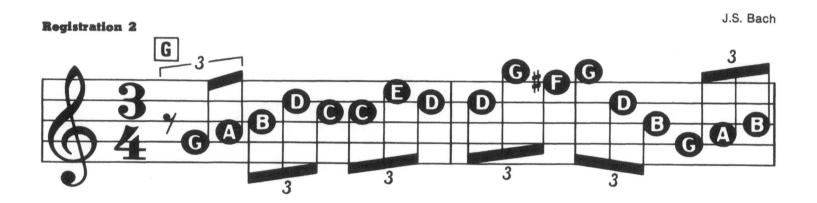

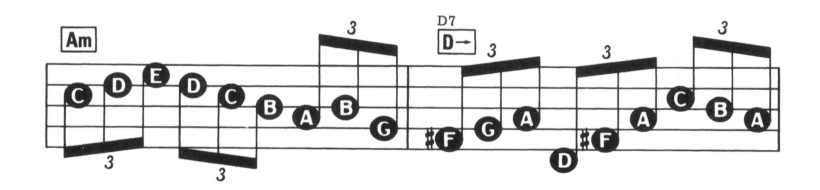

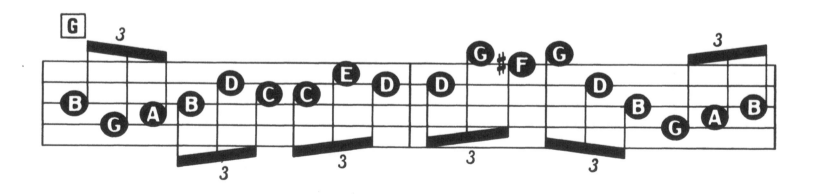

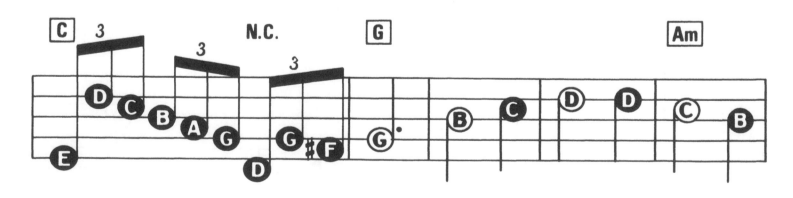

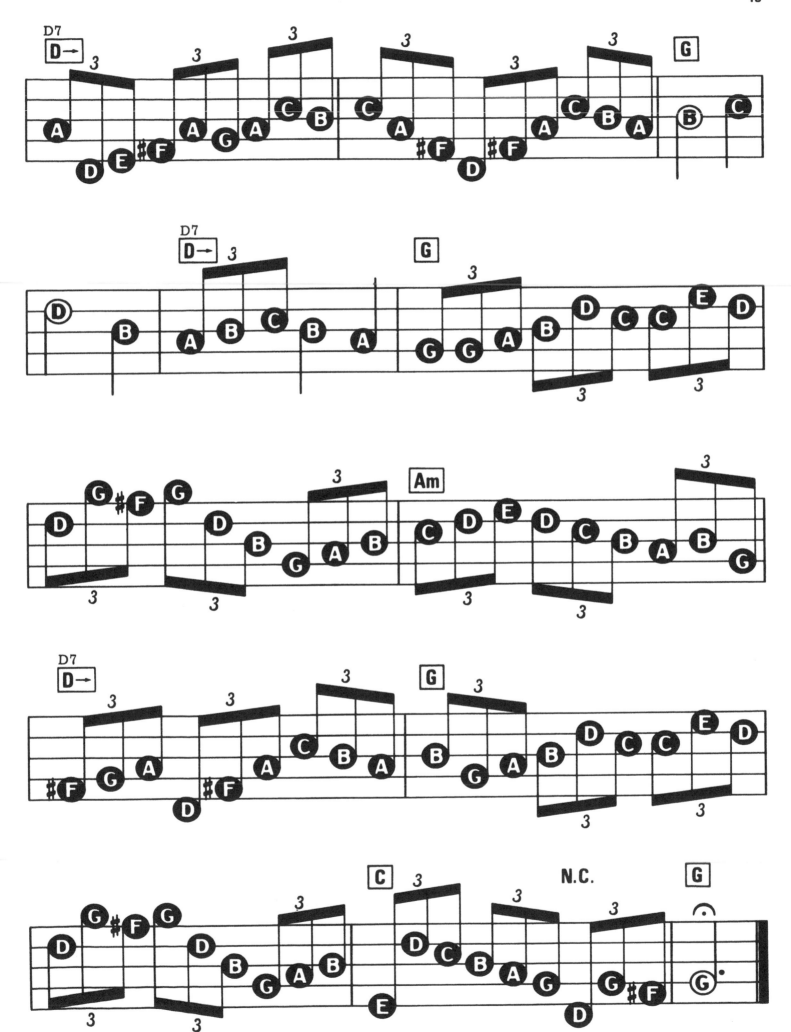

Largo
(From New World Symphony)
(De la Sinfonia del Nuevo Mundo)

A. Dvorak

Registration 2

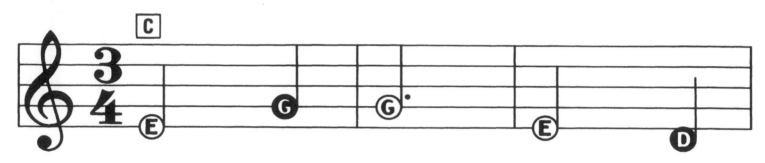

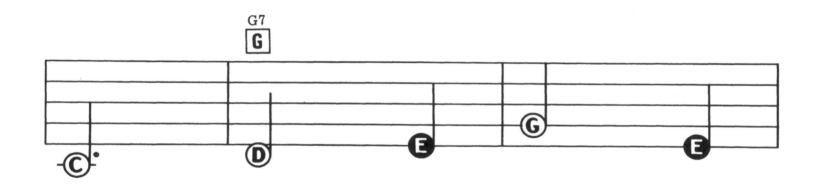

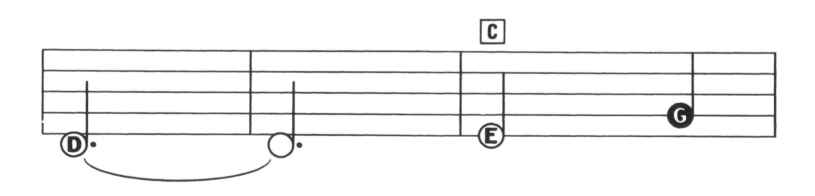

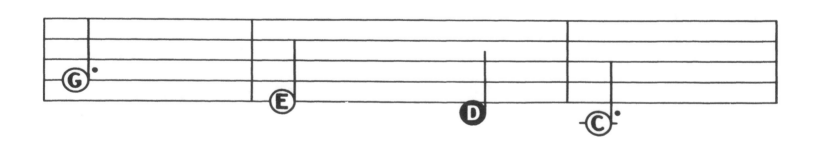

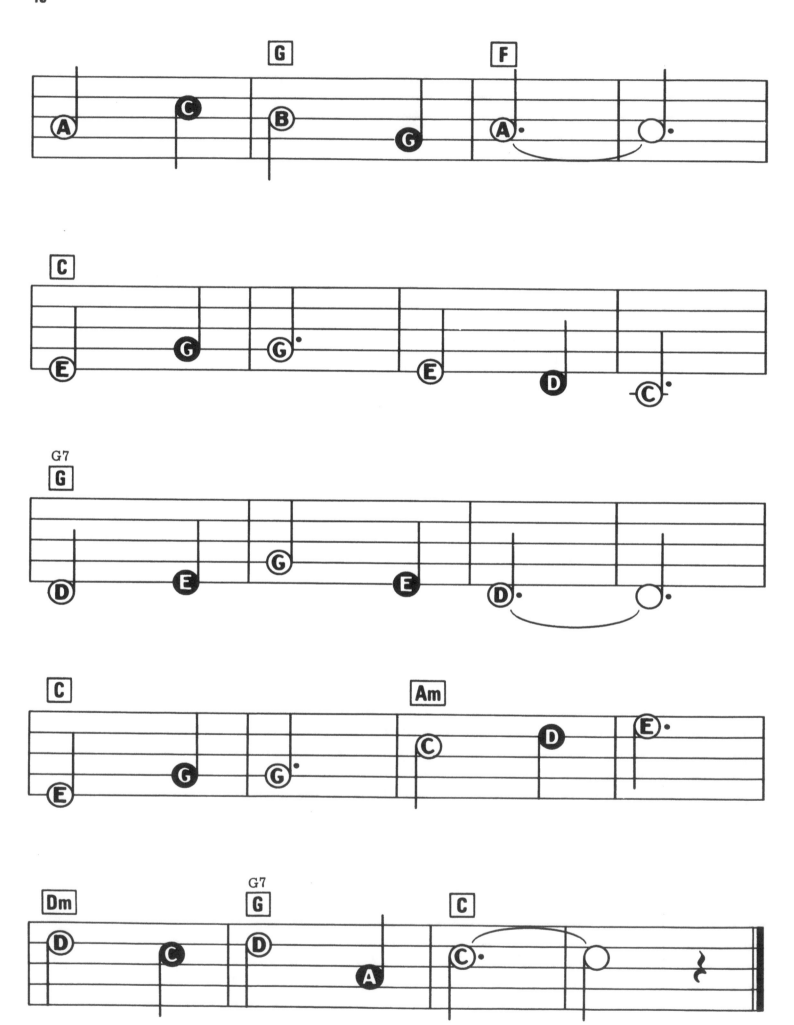

Liebestraum
(Sueño de Amor)

Franz Liszt

Registration 10

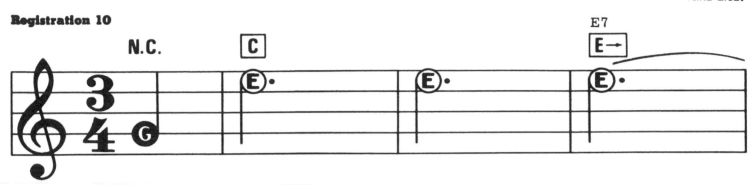

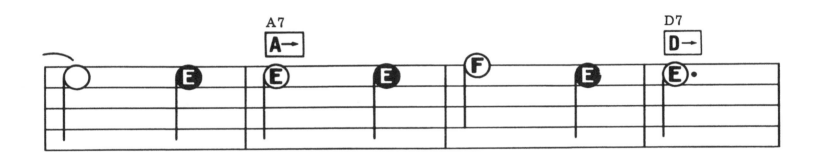

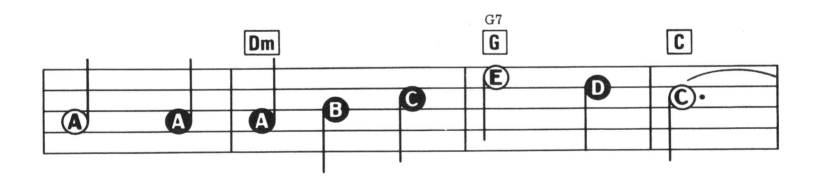

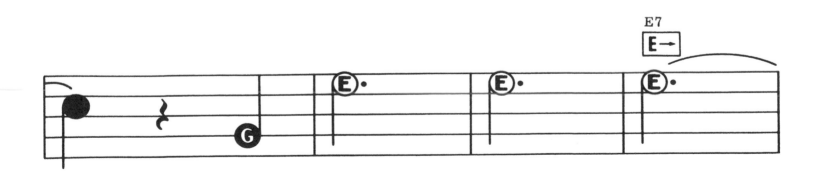

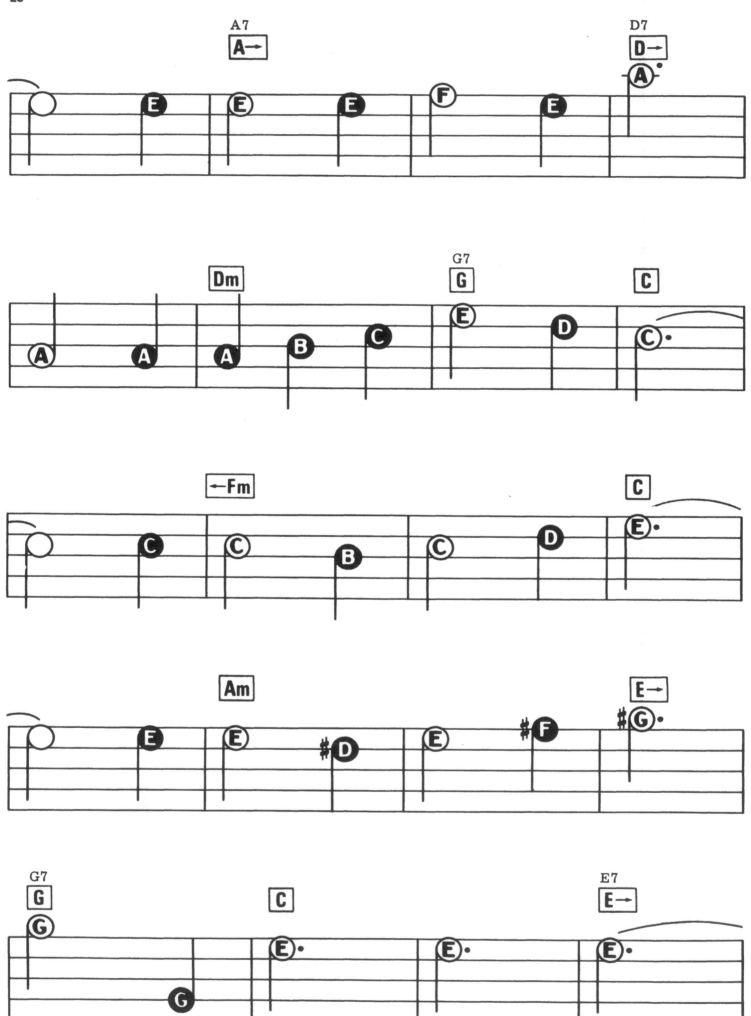

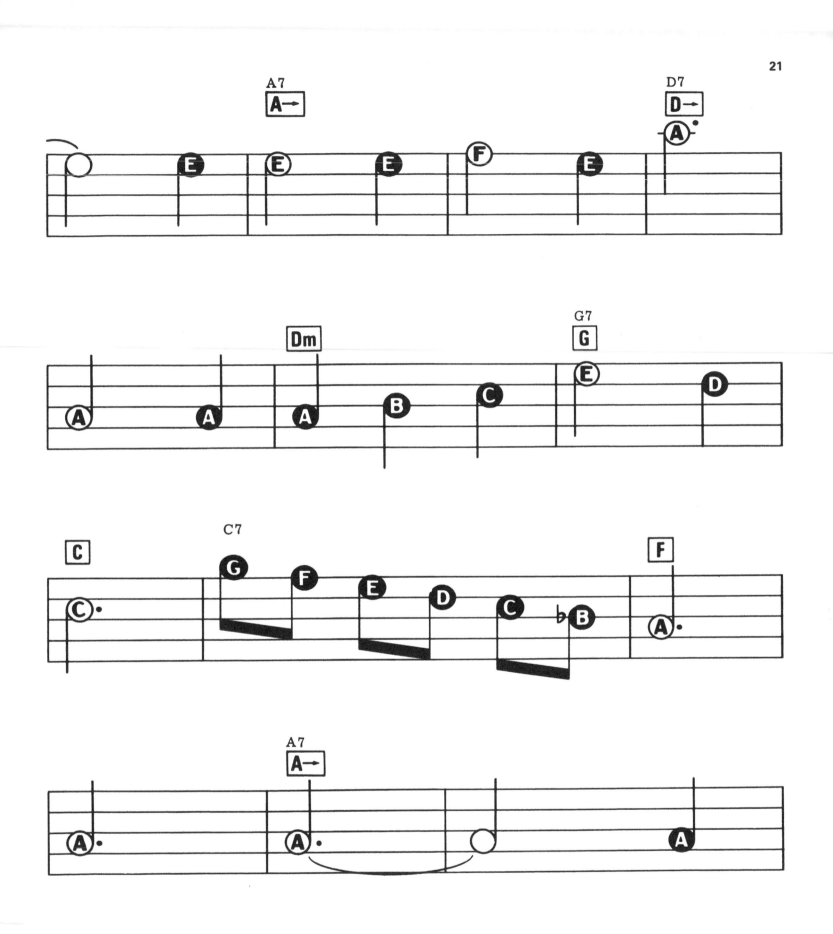

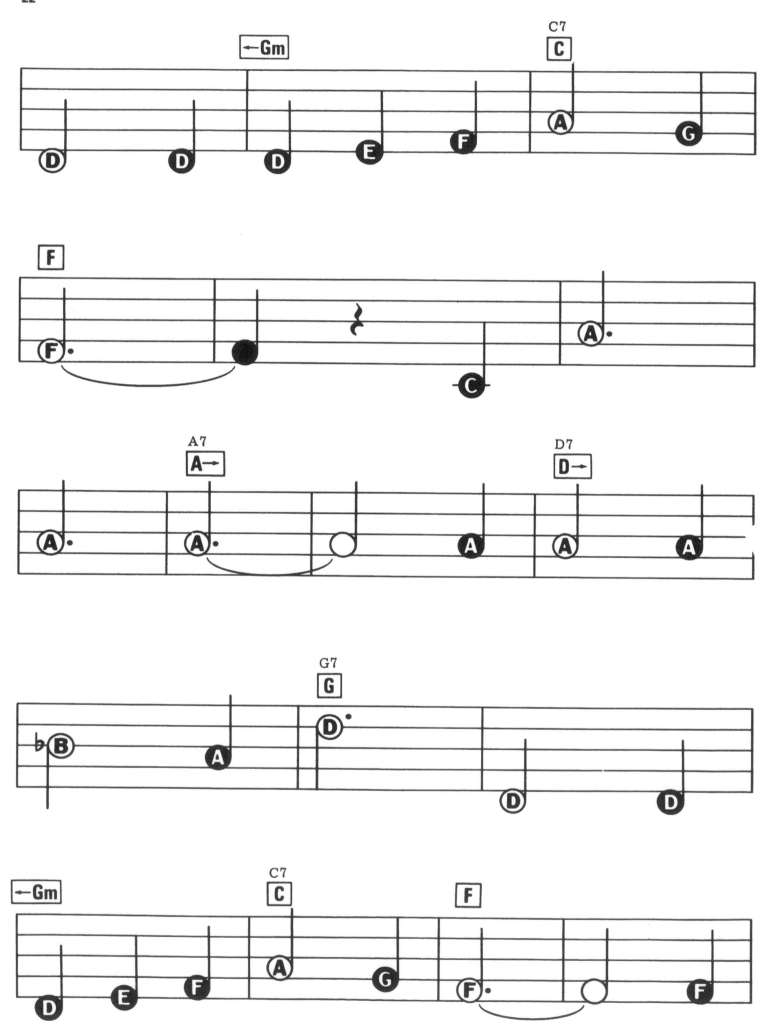

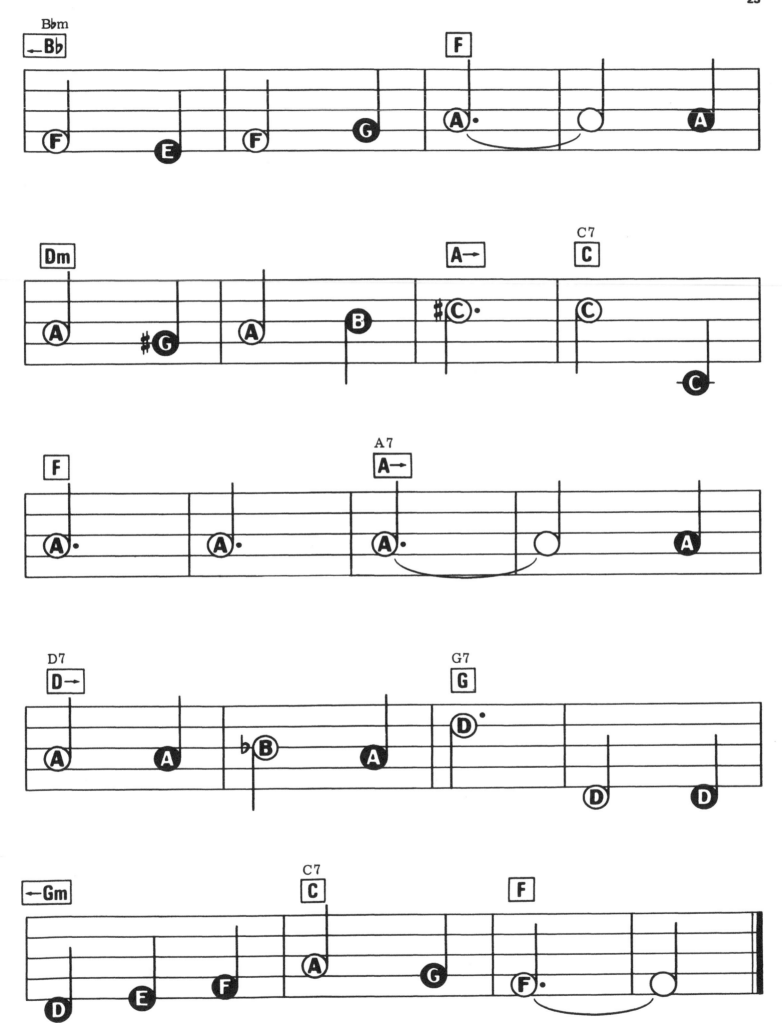

Minuet In G
(Minueto)

Registration 8

J.S. Bach

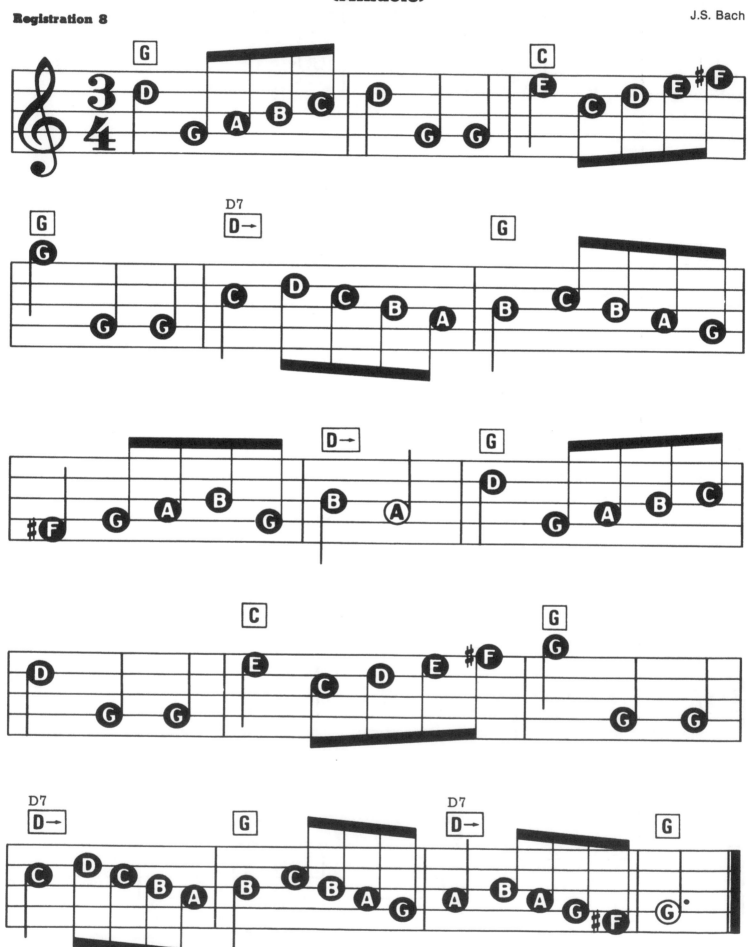

Moonlight Sonata
(Claro de Luna)

Ludwig von Beethoven

Registration 4

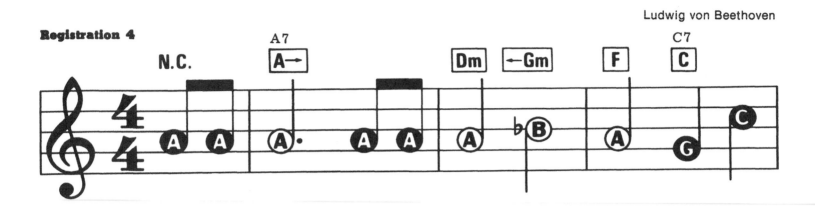

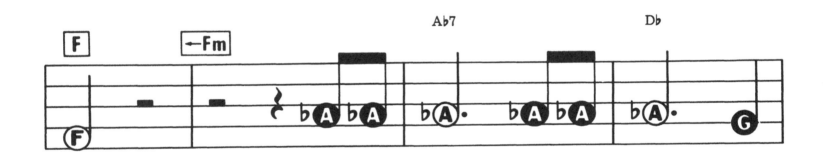

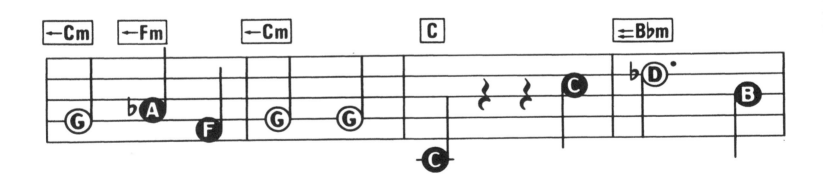

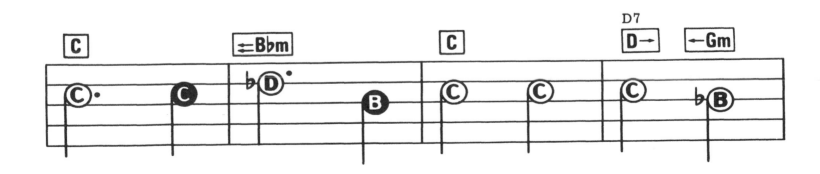

26

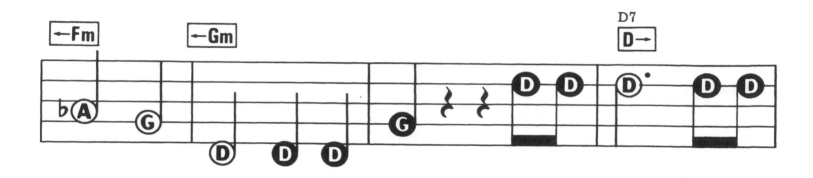

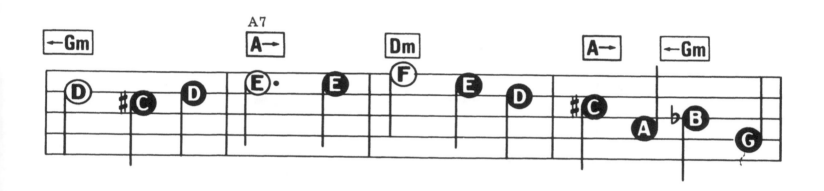

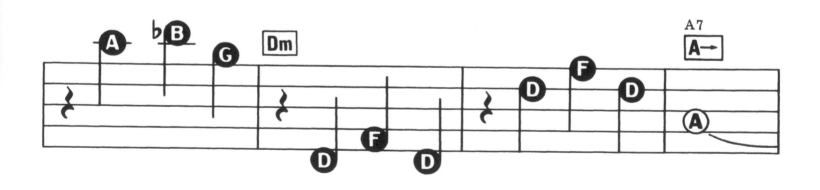

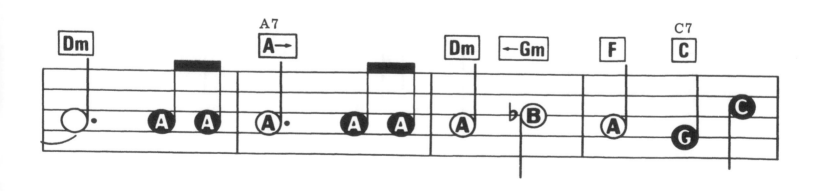

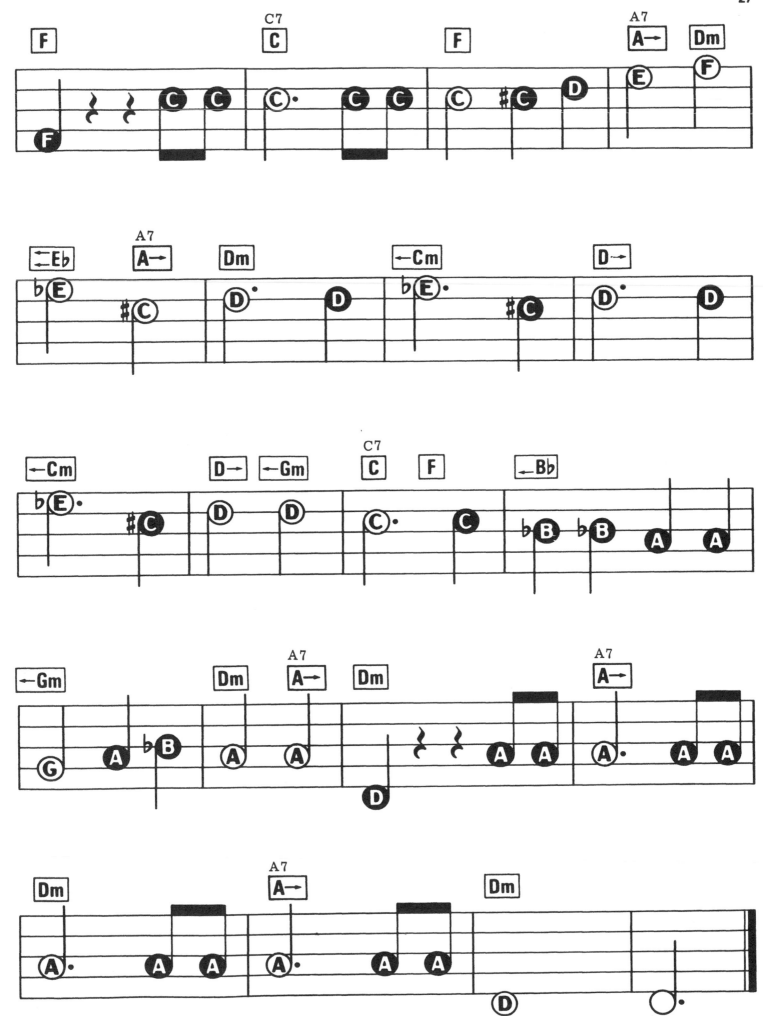

Polonaise, Opus 53
(Polenesa)

F. Chopin

Registration 5

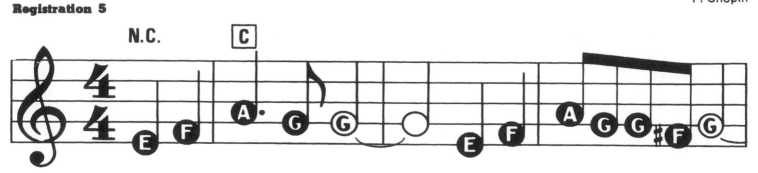

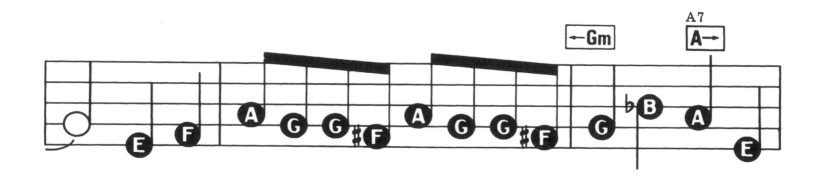

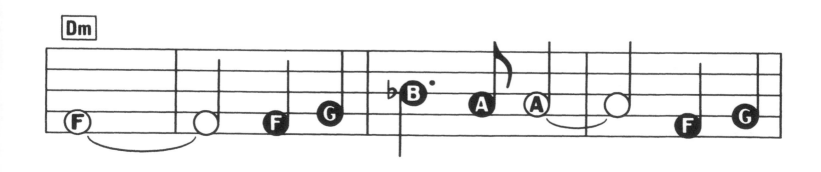

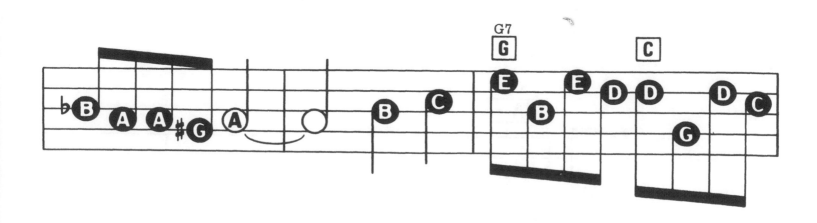

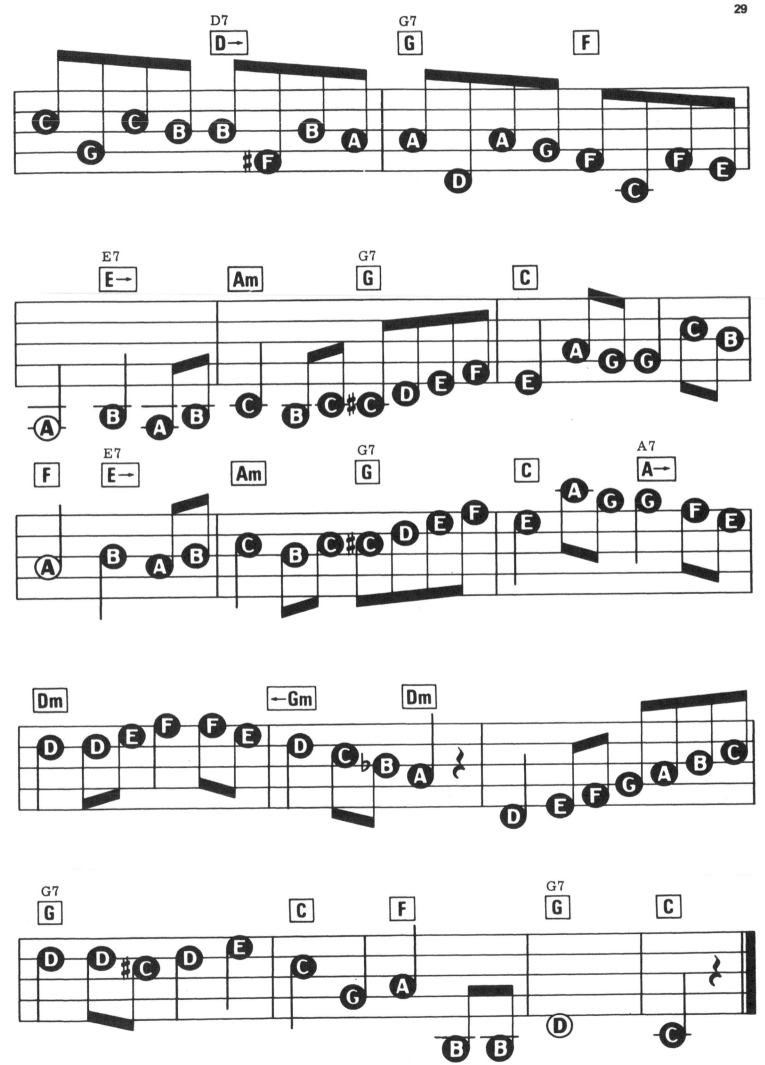

Sonata No.8 in C Minor
(Sonata Patética)

Ludwig von Beethoven

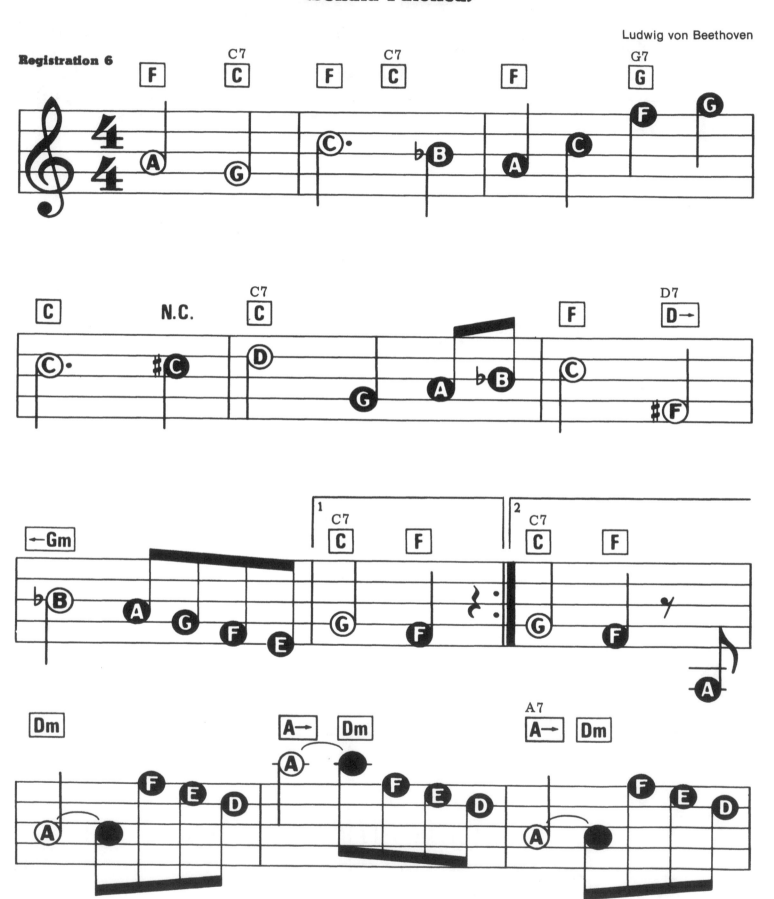

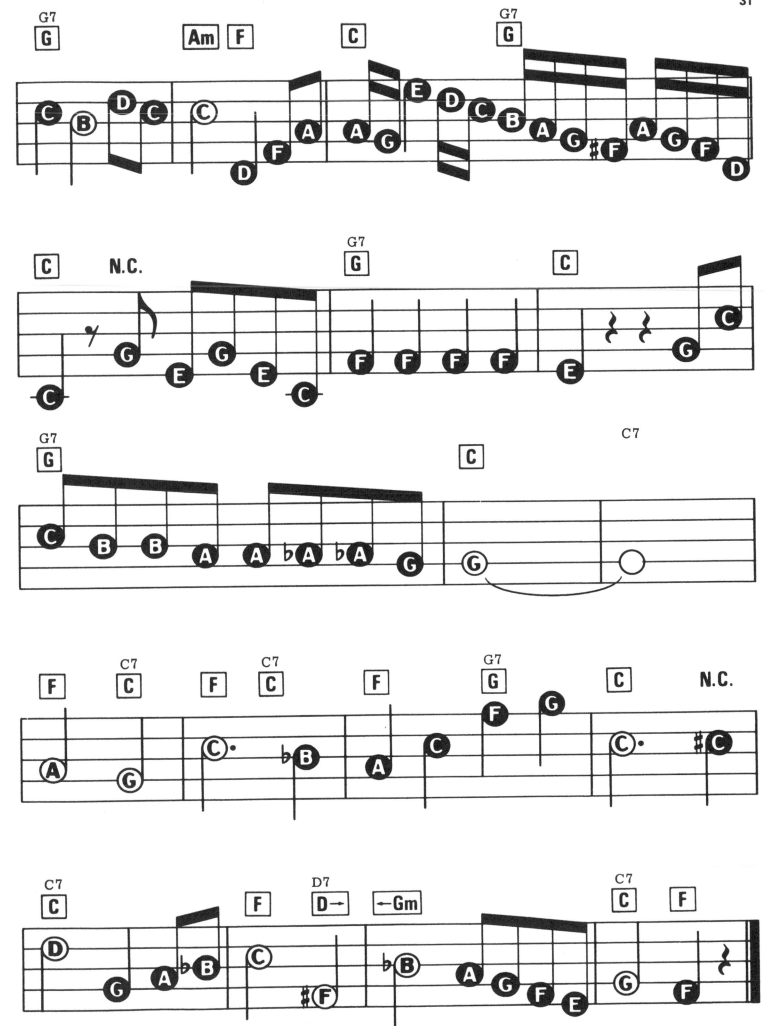

Sonata Pastoral
(Andante de la Sonata Pastoral)

Ludwig von Beethoven

Registration 6

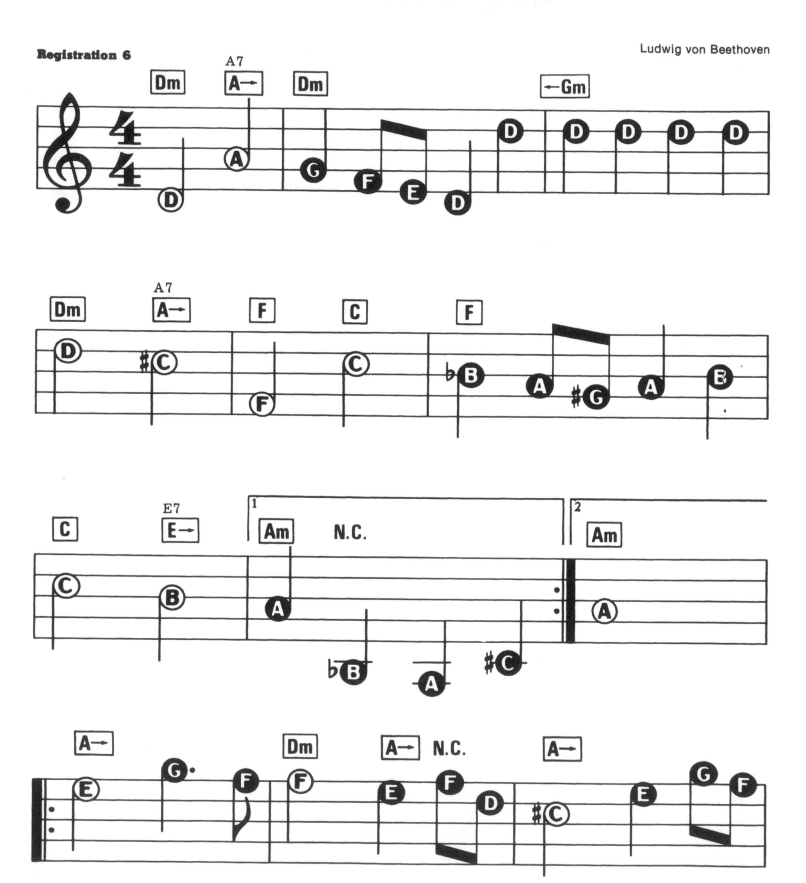

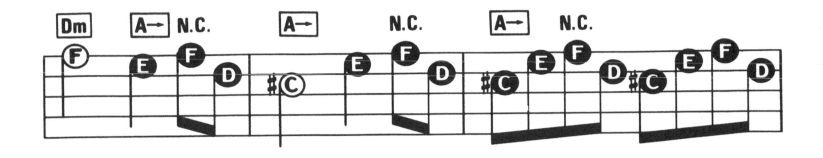

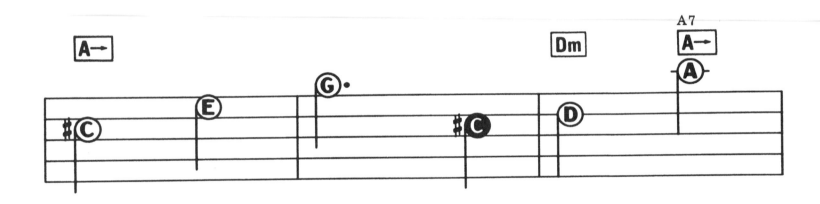

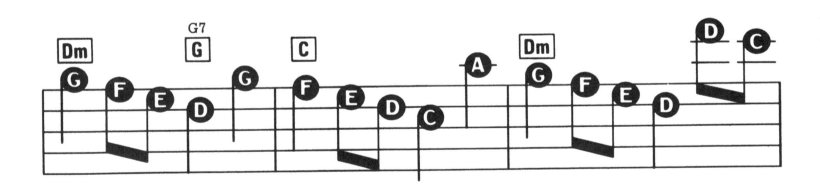

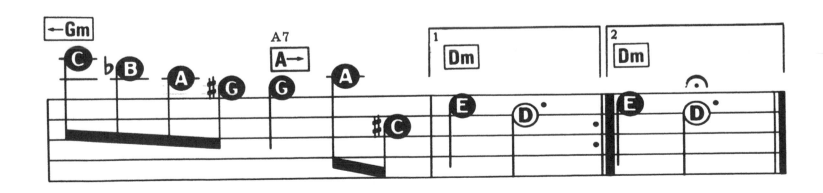

Theme From Swan Lake
(El Lago de los Cisnes)

Tchaikowsky

Registration 5

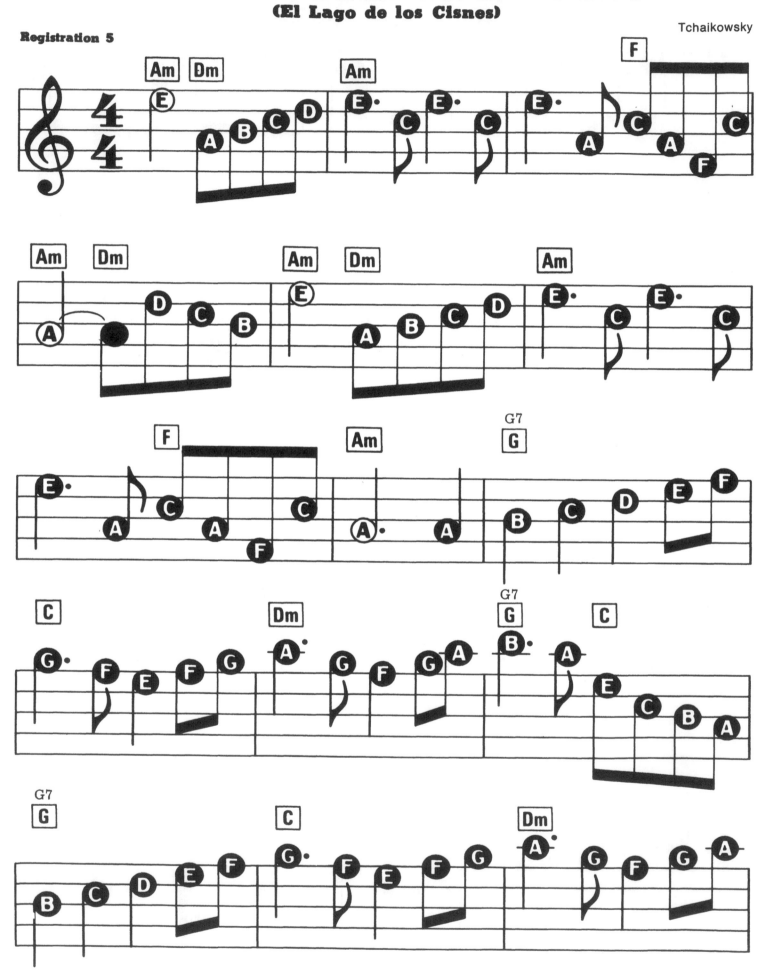

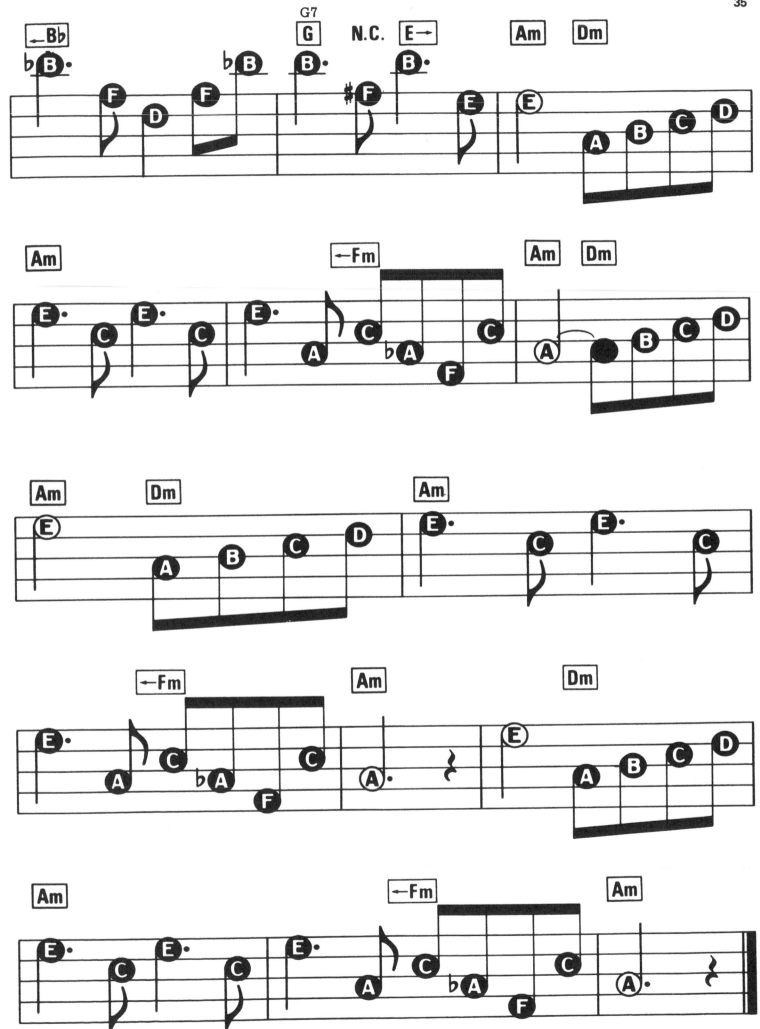

Theme From The Four Seasons
(Las Cuatro Estaciones)

Antonio Vivaldi

Registration 3

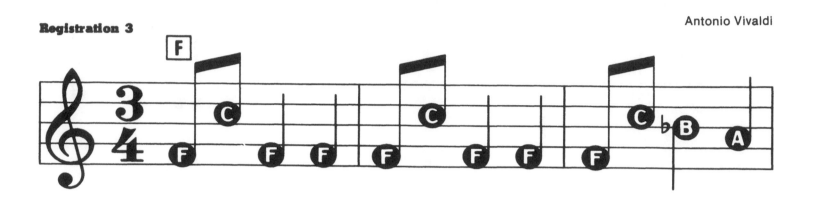

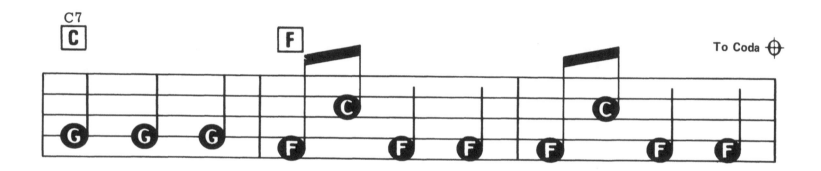

To Coda ⊕

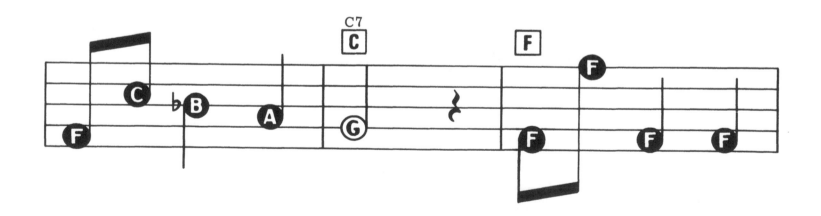

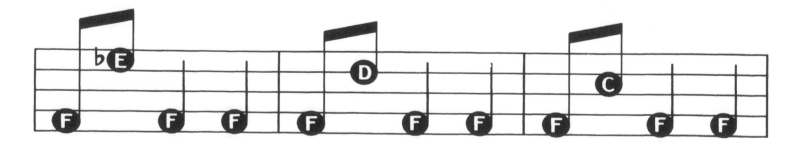

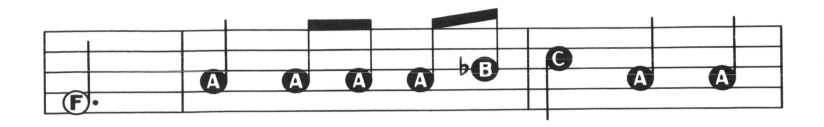

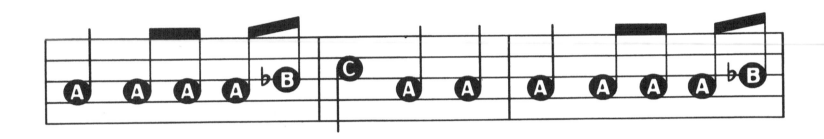

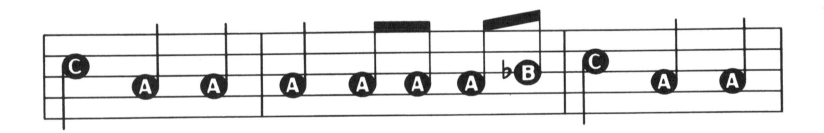

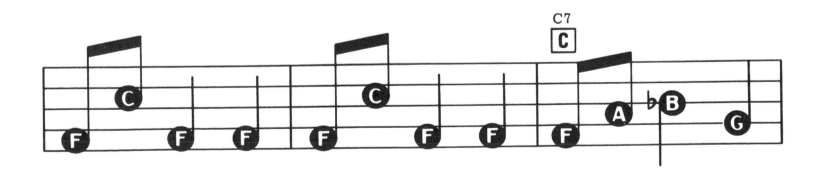

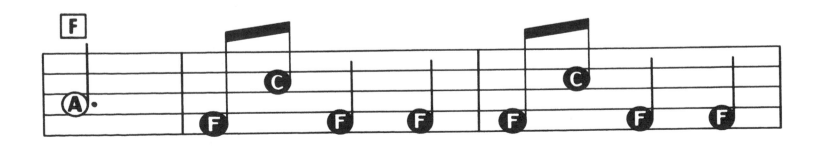

38

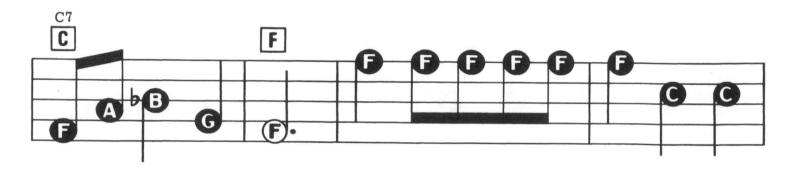

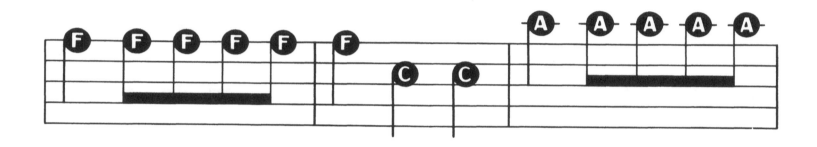

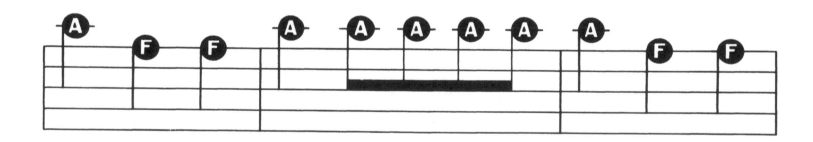

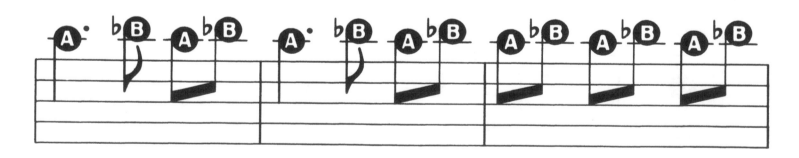

D.C. al Coda
(Return to beginning
Play to ✛ and skip to Coda) ✛ **CODA**

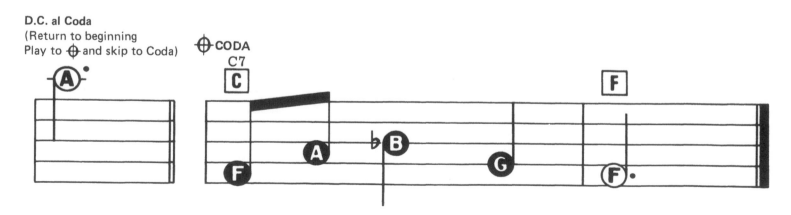

Unfinished Symphony
(Melodia Inacabada)

Franz Schubert

Registration 3

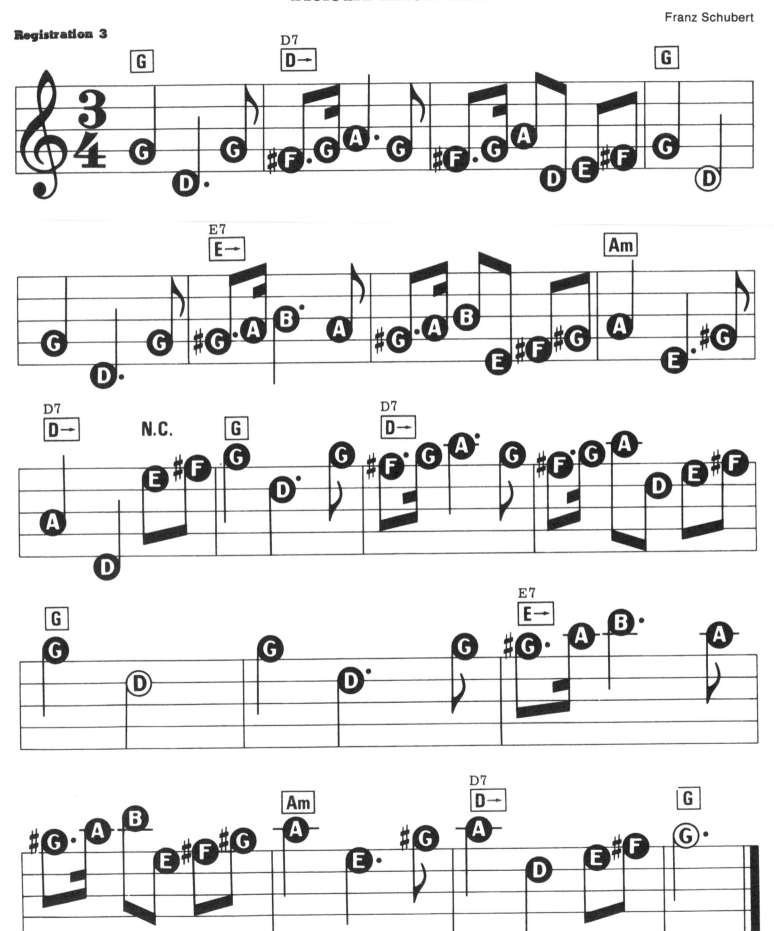

Waltz Of The Flowers
(Cascanueces)

Registration 9

Tchaikowsky

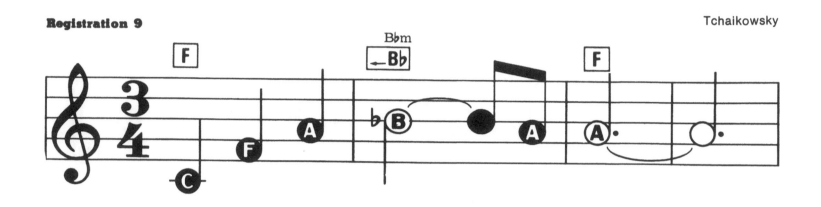

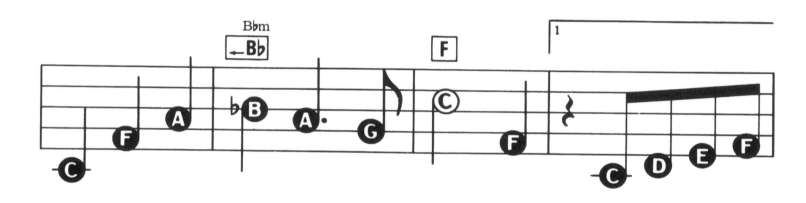

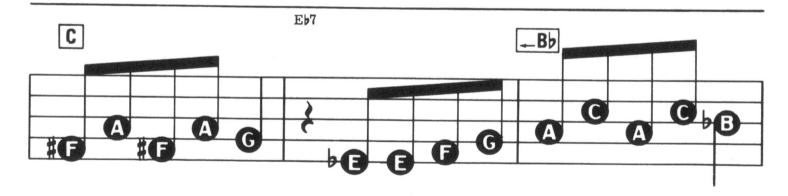

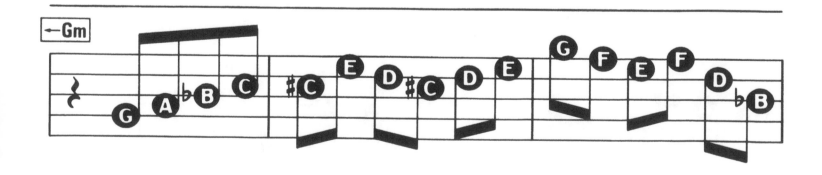

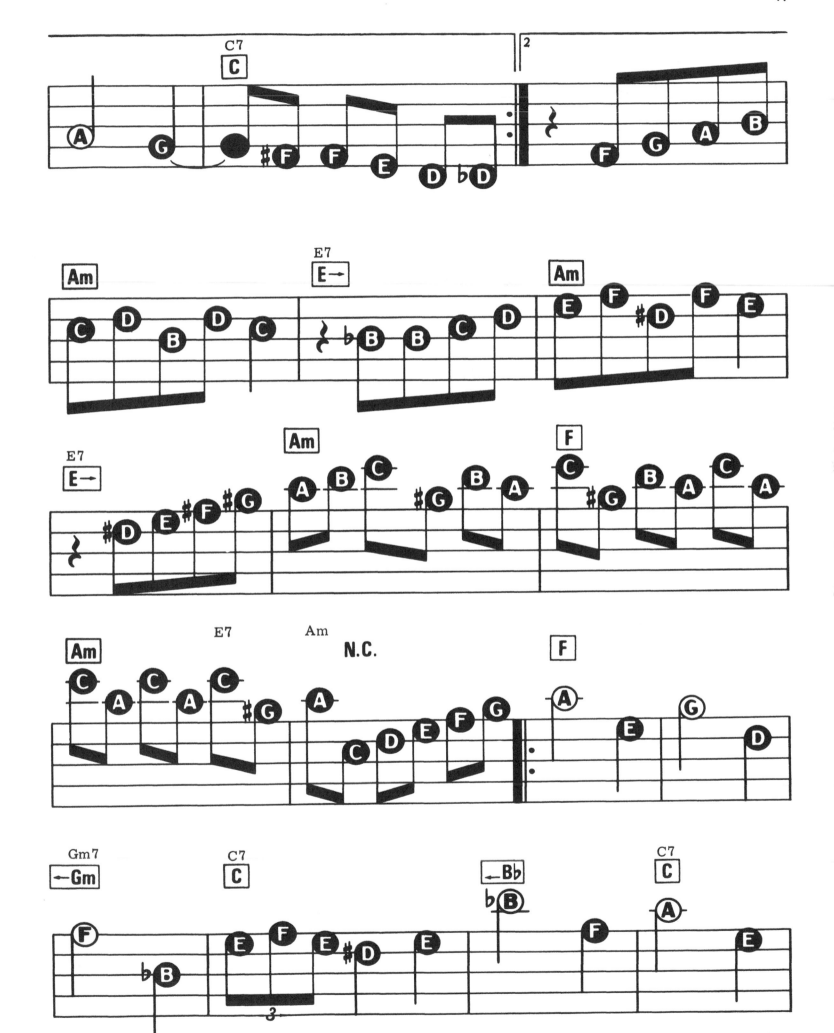

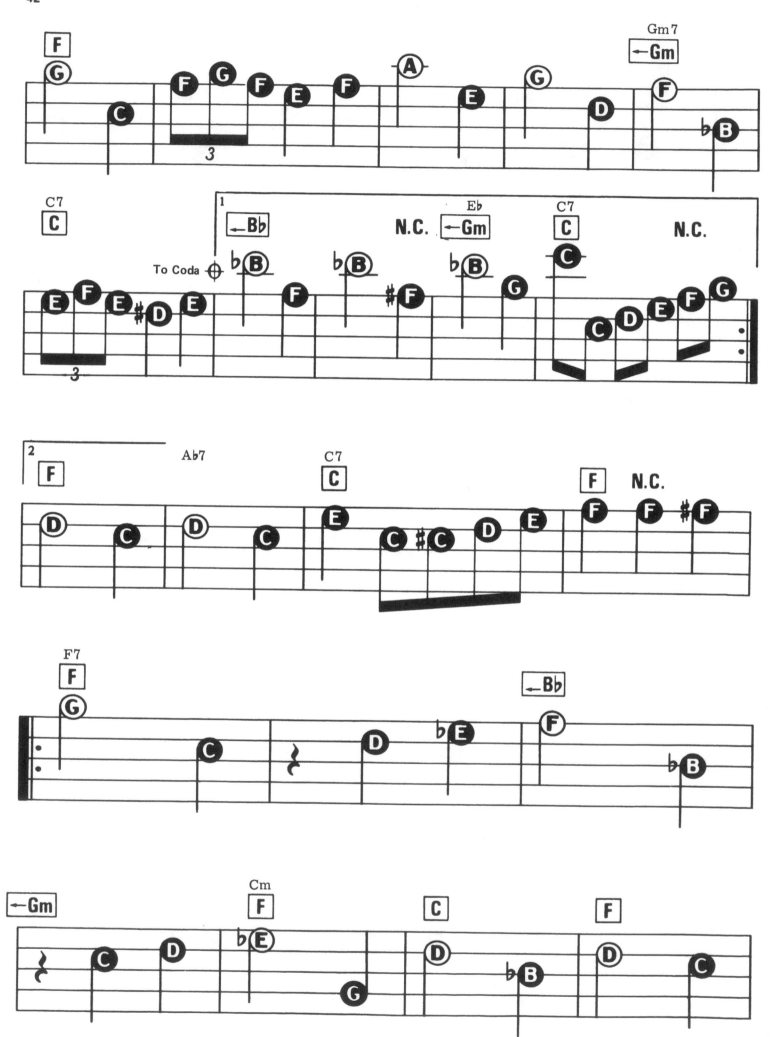

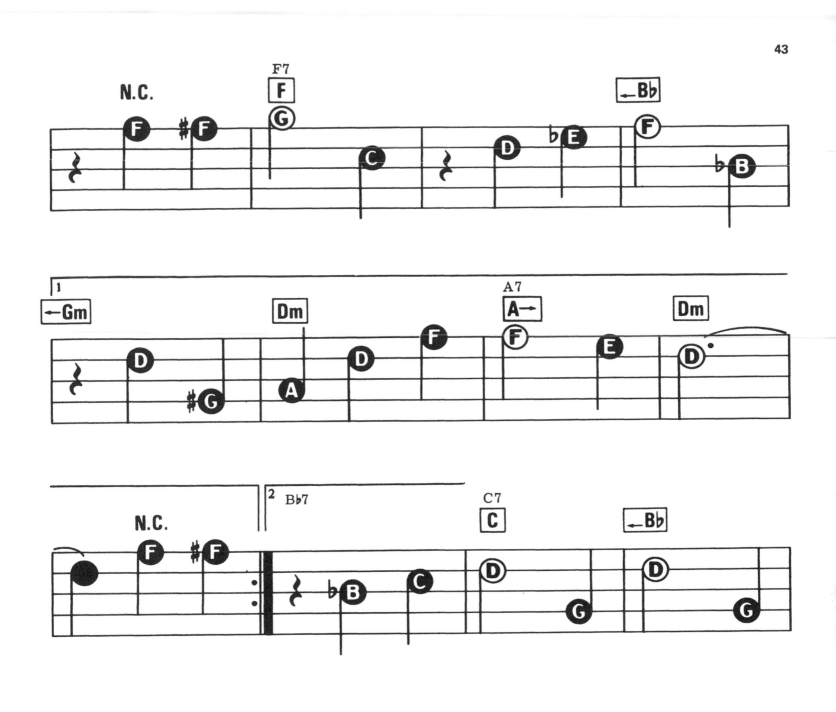

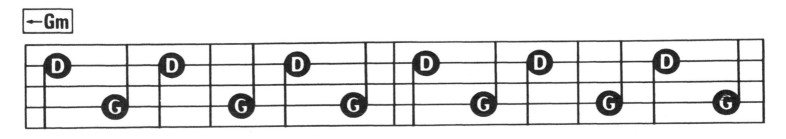

D.C. al Coda
(Return to beginning
Play to ⊕ and skip to Coda)

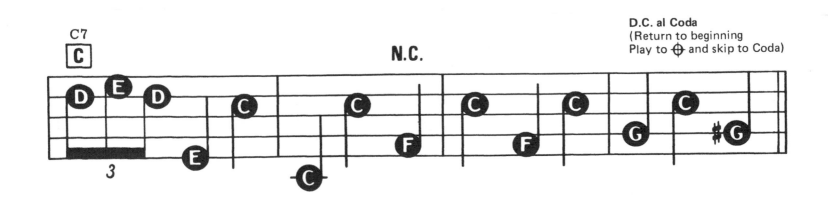

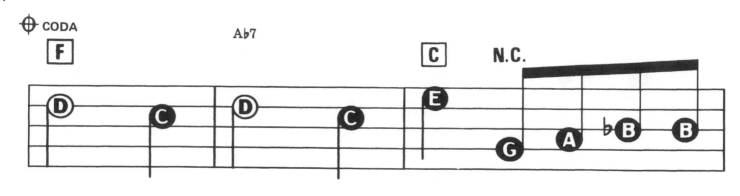

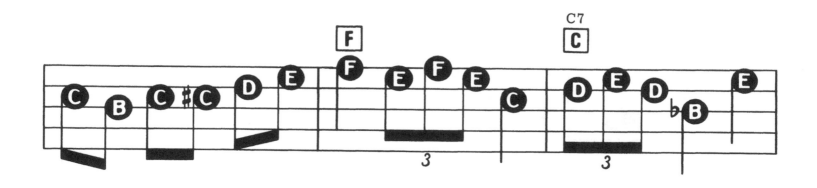

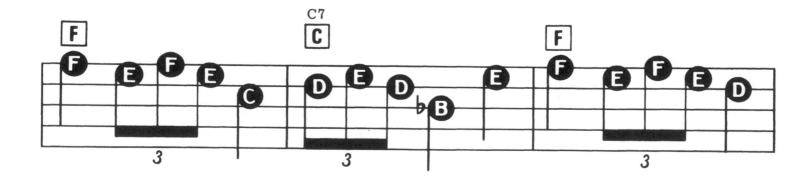

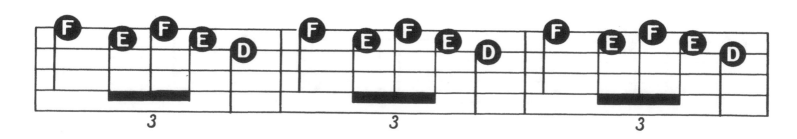

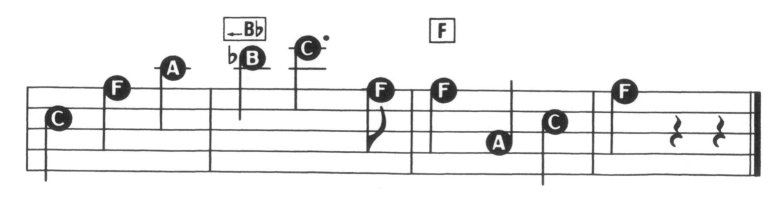

Wedding March
(Marcha Nupcial)

F. Mendelssohn

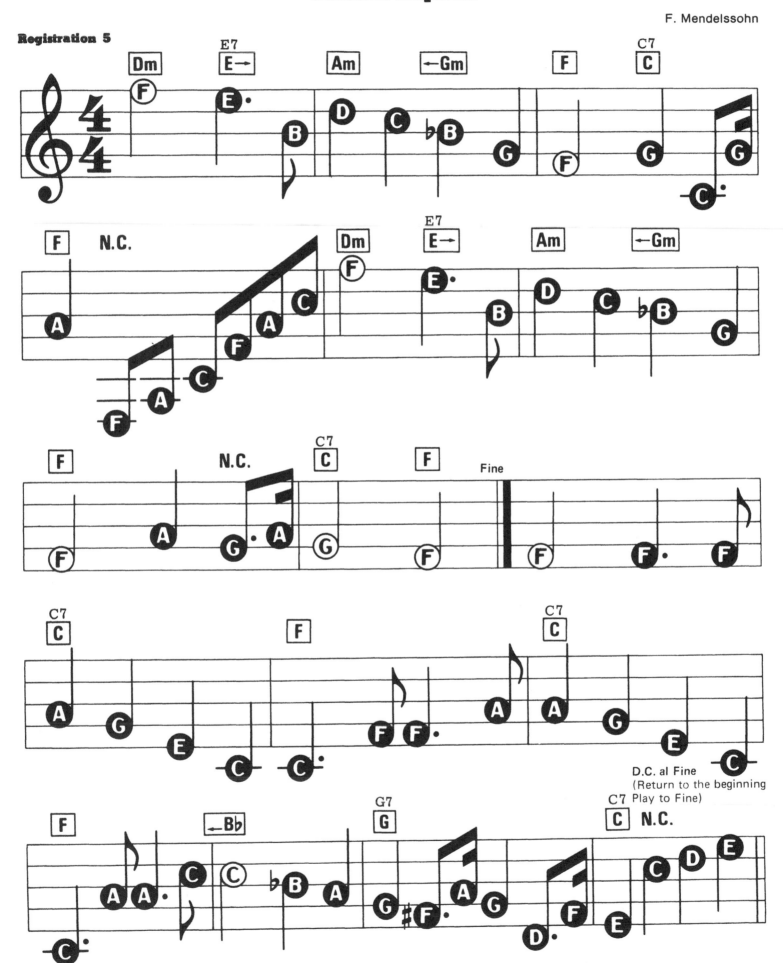

Music Basics

Fundamentos de Musica

THE MELODY (Right Hand)

The melody of a song appears as large lettered notes on a staff. The letter name corresponds to a key on the keyboard of an organ.

LA MELODIA (mano derecha)

La melodía de una canción se halla escrita mediante notas grandes en un pentagrama. Los nombres de las letras, que se hallan dentro de las notas, corresponden a las teclas en el teclado del órgano.

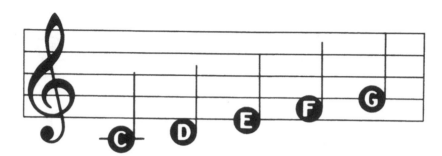

ACCOMPANIMENT (Left Hand)

The arrangements in this series have been written for all types of chord accompaniment.

1 One button (chord organ) or one-key chords.

2 Three-note (triad) chords.

3 Conventional, or standard chord positions.

Chord names, called chord symbols, appear above the melody line as either a boxed symbol [C]

or as an alternate chord (C7)

or both C7 [C]

1 For chord organ or one-key chords, play whichever chord name is on your unit.

2 If you are playing triad chords, follow the boxed symbols. A triad chord is played like this:

EL ACOMPAÑAMIENTO (mano izquierda)

Las adaptaciones en esta serie han sido escritas para todos los tipos de acompañamiento.

1 Acordes de un botón o una tecla.

2 Acordes de tres notas (tríada).

3 Acordes de posiciones convencionales.

Los nombres de los acordes, que se llaman símbolos de acordes, están escritos encima de la melodía en un cuadrado [C]

o como un acorde sustitutivo (C7)

o ambos C7 [C]

1 Para órganos con acordes mediante una tecla o un botón, toque el nombre de la letra que se halla escrito en su órgano.

2 Si toca acordes de tríada, use los acordes en los cuadrados. Un acorde de tríada se toca así:

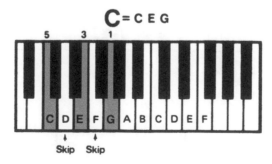

- Place your little finger on the key which has the same letter name as the chord.

- Skip a white key and place your middle finger on the next white key.

- Skip another white key and place your thumb on the next white key.

- Coloque su dedo 5 (meñique) en la tecla que tiene la misma letra que el acorde.

- Sáltese una tecla blanca y coloque su dedo 3 (medio) en la próxima tecla blanca.

- Sáltese otra tecla blanca y coloque su dedo 1 (pulgar) en la próxima tecla blanca.

In some cases, there is an ARROW to the **left** or to the **right** of the chord name.

The arrow indicates moving one of the triad notes either to the **left** or to the **right** on the keyboard.

To understand this, first think of a chord symbol as having three sections, representing the three notes of the chord.

En algunos casos, hay flechas a la izquierda o a la derecha del símbolo del acorde.

La flecha(s) indica una alternación de la tríada, a la **derecha** o a la **izquierda.**

Para comprenderlo, primero, piense que el símbolo de un acorde tiene tres secciones representando las tres notas del acorde.

An ARROW is positioned next to the chord letter in one of these sections, indicating which of the three notes to change. For example:

- An arrow to the left means to move a note of the chord **down** (left) to the next adjacent key.

Las FLECHAS están colocadas en una o más de estas secciones indicando cual de las tres se cambia. Por ejemplo:

● Una flecha a la izquierda de la letra significa mover una nota del acorde **hacia abajo** (a la izquierda) de la próxima tecla adyacente.

In this example where the arrow is in the **lower left**, or "1" position, move the first note "B" **down** to the black key B♭.

En este ejemplo, la flecha está a la **izquierda,** o en la primera posición, indicando mover la primera nota "B" **hacia abajo** a la tecla negra, B♭.

- An arrow to the right means to move a note of the chord **up** (right) to the next adjacent key.

● Una flecha a la derecha de la letra significa mover una nota del acorde **hacia arriba** (a la derecha) de la próxima tecla adyacente.

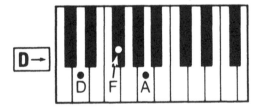

In this example where the arrow is in the **middle**, or "2" position, move the middle note **up** to the black key F♯.

En este ejemplo, la flecha está a la **mitad,** o en la segunda posición, indicando mover la segunda nota "F" **hacia arriba** a la tecla negra, F♯.

3 If you are playing standard chord positions, play the chord in the boxed symbol, unless an alternate chord is indicated. Play alternate chords whenever possible.

For your reference, a Chord Speller Chart of standard chord positions appears in the back of this book.

3 Si toca acordes de posiciones convencionales, toque el acorde cuadrado, a menos que haya un acorde sustituto. Toque el acorde sustituto cuando se indique.

Al final de esta inserción aparece para su referencia un Cuadro Descriptivo de Acordes con las inversiones de los acordes que se utilizan normalmente.

REGISTRATION AND RHYTHM

A Registration number is shown above the music for each song. This number corresponds to the same number on the Registration Guide which appears on the inside front cover of this book. The Registration numbers also correspond to the numbers on the E-Z Play TODAY Registration Guides that are available for many brands of organs. See your organ dealer for the details.

You may wish to select your own favorite registration or perhaps experimant with different voice combinations. Then add an automatic rhythm...and HAVE FUN.

REGISTRACION Y RITMO

Al principio de cada canción aparece un Número de Registro. Dicho número se corresponde con el mismo número en la Guia de Registros incluida en el interior de la portada de este libro. Los números de Registro tambien se corresponden con las Guias de Registros de la serie E-Z Play TODAY específicas para muchas de las marcas de órganos electrónicos. Consulte a su proveedor de música para una mayor información.

Es muy posible quie Ud. desee seleccionar su propia registración, o, quizá, experimentar con diferentes combinaciones. En este caso, añada un ritmo automático...y DIVIERTASE.

Chord Speller Chart
of Standard Chord Positions

Cuadro Descriptivo de Acordes
Posiciones Standard

For those who play standard chord positions, all chords used in the E-Z Play TODAY music arrangements are shown here in their most commonly used chord positions. Suggested fingering is also indicated, but feel free to use alternate fingering.

Todos los acordes en las adaptaciones de la música E-Z se muestran aquí en sus inversiones (posiciones) utilizadas más comúnmente. Se le indica también la digitación apropiada, pero si lo desea, utilice una digitación alternativa.

Chord Family Abbrev. (Abreviaturas del conjunto de los acordes)	MAJOR (MAYOR)	MINOR (MENOR) (m)	SEVENTH (SEPTIMA) (7)	MINOR SEVENTH (SEPTIMA MENOR) (m7)
C	5 2 1 G-C-E	5 2 1 G-C-E♭	5 3 2 1 G-B♭-C-E	5 3 2 1 G-B♭-C-E♭
D♭	5 2 1 A♭-D♭-F	5 2 1 A♭-D♭-E	5 3 2 1 A♭-B-D♭-F	5 3 2 1 A♭-B-D♭-E
D	5 3 1 F♯-A-D	5 2 1 A-D-F	5 3 2 1 F♯-A-C-D	5 3 2 1 A-C-D-F
E♭	5 3 1 G-B♭-E♭	5 3 1 G♭-B♭-E♭	5 3 2 1 G-B♭-D♭-E♭	5 3 2 1 G♭-B♭-D♭-E♭
E	5 3 1 G♯-B-E	5 3 1 G-B-E	5 3 2 1 G♯-B-D-E	5 3 2 1 G-B-D-E
F	4 2 1 A-C-F	4 2 1 A♭-C-F	5 3 2 1 A-C-E♭-F	5 3 2 1 A♭-C-E♭-F
F♯	4 2 1 F♯-A♯-C♯	4 2 1 F♯-A-C♯	5 3 2 1 F♯-A♯-C♯-E	5 3 2 1 F♯-A-C♯-E
G	5 3 1 G-B-D	5 3 1 G-B♭-D	5 3 2 1 G-B-D-F	5 3 2 1 G-B♭-D-F
A♭	4 2 1 A♭-C-E♭	4 2 1 A♭-B-E♭	5 3 2 1 A♭-C-E♭-G♭	5 3 2 1 A♭-B-E♭-G♭
A	4 2 1 A-C♯-E	4 2 1 A-C-E	5 4 2 1 G-A-C♯-E	5 4 2 1 G-A-C-E
B♭	4 2 1 B♭-D-F	4 2 1 B♭-D♭-F	5 4 2 1 A♭-B♭-D-F	5 4 2 1 A♭-B♭-D♭-F
B	5 2 1 F♯-B-D♯	5 2 1 F♯-B-D	5 3 2 1 F♯-A-B-D♯	5 3 2 1 F♯-A-B-D